SCHOLASTIC
News
Nonfiction Readers

The Sun

by
Melanie Chrismer

Children's Press®
A Division of Scholastic Inc.
New York Toronto London Auckland Sydney
Mexico City New Delhi Hong Kong
Danbury, Connecticut

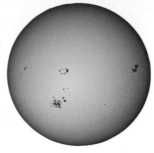

These content vocabulary word builders
are for grades 1-2.

Consultants: Daniel D. Kelson, Ph.D.
Carnegie Observatories
Pasadena, CA
and
Andrew Fraknoi
Astronomy Department, Foothill College

Curriculum Specialist: Linda Bullock

Photo Credits:

Photographs © 2005: Corbis Images: 1, 5 bottom left, 7 (Paul A. Souders), 4 top, 5 top right, 17 (Craig Tuttle); Holiday Film Corp.: back cover; NASA: cover; Photo Researchers, NY: 2, 5 top left, 13 (John Chumack), 19 (Gregory G. Dimijian), 5 bottom right, 15 (Scharmer et al, Royal Swedish Academy of Sciences), 4 bottom left, 11 (Detlev van Ravenswaay); Stone/Getty Images/Doug Armand: 4 bottom right, 9; Tom Stack & Associates, Inc./NOAA/TSADO: 23.

Book Design: Simonsays Design!
Library of Congress Cataloging-in-Publication Data

Chrismer, Melanie.
     The sun / by Melanie Chrismer.
         p. cm. – (Scholastic news nonfiction readers)
     Includes bibliographical references and index.
     ISBN 0-516-24914-2 (lib. bdg.)
     1. Sun–Juvenile literature. I. Title. II. Series.
     QB521.5.C57 2005
     523.7–dc22

                                                                     2005002421

CONTENTS

WORD HUNT

Look for these words as you read. They will be in **bold**.

atmosphere
(**at**-muhss-fihr)

solar system
(**soh**-lur **siss**-tuhm)

4

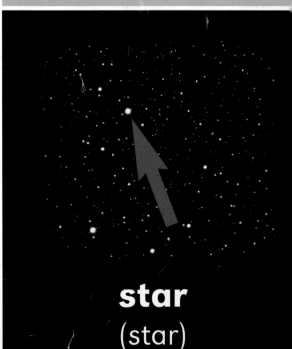

star
(star)

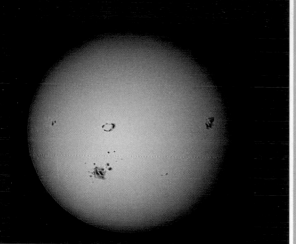

photosphere
(**foh**-toh-sfihr)

radiation
(ray-dee-**ay**-shuhn)

Sun
(suhn)

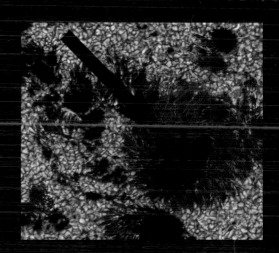

sunspot
(**suhn**-spot)

The Sun!

The **Sun** comes up
every day.

You can see it come up.

You can watch it go down.

Can you visit the Sun?

No. Let's see why.

The Sun always comes up in the East.
It goes down, or sets, in the West.

The Sun is a **star**.

Stars are big balls of hot gases.

The Sun looks bigger than other stars.

It is not. It is just closer to us. Other stars are farther away.

star

Stars look close, but they are far away.

The Sun is the biggest object in our **solar system**.

All of the other objects in our solar system travel around the Sun.

The planets are as small as grains of sand next to the Sun.

Sun

Earth

The Sun is very hot.

The Sun's surface is about 10,000 degrees!

The surface of the sun is called the **photosphere**.

This is the surface of the Sun.

13

The photosphere has dark dots called **sunspots**.

Never look at the Sun to hunt for sunspots.

The Sun is very bright. It can hurt your eyes.

Sunspots are not as hot as other parts of the Sun.

The Sun gives Earth light and heat called **radiation**.

Even Earth's blue sky is from the Sun.

The blue comes from sunlight shining in our **atmosphere**.

The Sun can warm up a place even if it is cold.

The Sun is too hot and too bright to visit.

It is 93 million miles away from Earth.

That is very far away, but it is just right for life on Earth!

Life on Earth depends on the Sun.

THE SUN

IN OUR SOLAR SYSTEM

Sun

Venus

Saturn

Earth

Neptune

YOUR NEW WORDS

atmosphere (**at**-muhss-fihr) the gases around a planet

photosphere (**foh**-toh-sfihr) the surface of the Sun

radiation (ray-dee-**ay**-shuhn) waves of energy and light

solar system (**soh**-lur **siss**-tuhm) the group of planets, moons, and other things that travel around the Sun

star (star) a ball of hot gases that gives off light and heat

sun (suhn) the biggest object in our solar system

sunspot (**suhn**-spot) a dark area on the surface of the Sun

The Sun Is an Amazing Star!

A day is how long it takes a planet or star to turn one time.

One day on the Sun is about 650 hours. This is about 27 days on Earth.

The Sun has no moons.

The Sun is a star, not a planet.

One million Earths could fit inside the Sun.

INDEX

FIND OUT MORE

Book:

The Sun: Center of the Solar System
Michael D. Cole, Enslow Publishers, Inc., 2001

Website:

Sun Information and Pictures
http://starchild.gsfc.nasa.gov/docs/StarChild/
solar_system_level1/sun.html

MEET THE AUTHOR:

Melanie Chrismer grew up near NASA in Houston, Texas. She loves math and science and has written 12 books for children. To write her books, she visited NASA where she floated in the zero-gravity trainer called the Vomit Comet. She says, "it is the best roller coaster ever!"